They're Your Kids Too

*The Single Father's Guide
to Defending Your Fatherhood
in a Broken Family
Law System*

by

Anne P. Mitchell,
Attorney at Law

Praise for They're Your Kids Too:

"In a divorce, nobody wins, but the kids in a divorce should not suffer. Kids need both parents. This book is an absolute MUST have for all men going through divorce with kids!"

- Bruce D.

They're Your Kids Too provides critical, relevant and thought-provoking information. It helped me in addressing and dealing with several critical issues.

- S.S., California

Your book was a blessing for my nephew. While he does not live in the St. Louis area, the information provided was invaluable in his fight to keep his children close. We can't thank you enough!

- Shawn's Aunt

I found the material in this book very informative. I even shared several excerpts with my family counselor and attorney. I only wish I had discovered the information prior to me ex-wife's antics regarding my little girl. Two thumbs up and a professional recommendation!

- Jeff T., ABR, CRS, NC Broker, Realtor, SRS

This is the best help guide you can ever get for help with your kids and/or divorce. Loads of great information and well worth buying.

- Mike

This book has been a great supplement to all the other research I have done. It is a priceless resource...well worth the time to read!!

- David H.

This was my guiding light which helped me get through a turbulent and stressful time with a great sense of peace.

- N.P.

Family support groups, law schools, and other institutions and organizations
wishing a bulk purchase price should contact info@dadsrights.org

Mitchell, Anne P.,
ISBN: 978-0-615-51443-7

Book Design by Steven Peterson

Printed in the United States of America

Distributed by ISIPP Publishing
Henderson, Nevada
www.IsippPublishing.com

This book is the distillation of decades of work and experience advocating for fathers and their children, both in and outside of court. My journey from impoverished inner-city child to Stanford Law School to national fathers' rights attorney was a long one, and made possible only with the encouragement and faith of many friends and colleagues along the way. In particular I would like to thank Larry Viola, Jim Knapp, and Gary Royce, attorneys at law, for providing me the ability to practice family law for fathers from the very moment that I graduated from law school; Paul Vixie, for both the technical and moral support that he provided as I ventured out on my own; and Frank Presto, Guy Kawasaki, and Tom Campbell, for their mentoring and friendship.

I dedicate this book to my amazing and wonderful children, Jessica and William, who are my greatest inspiration, and my daily affirmation of how important it is for fathers to be there for their children even after divorce; and to my own father, who insisted on that involvement in my own life in an era when divorced men were supposed to quietly fade away, and who passed away just as I was starting law school. I love you, Dad.

In memory of
William Francis Mitchell
1932 - 1989

Table of Contents

Chapter Three:
Parental Kidnapping: Prepare for it–Prevent it 37

Chapter Four:
Parental Alienation:
When "He Said, She Said"
Becomes "He's Gone, She Won" 47

Chapter Five:
Resources

A Note from Anne P. Mitchell, Author, Fathers' Rights Attorney and Founder of DadsRights.org

I'm so pleased that you have picked up this book. The very fact that you are reading it means that you are someone who truly cares about the well-being of the children with whom you are (or want to be) involved.

The odds are good that you are either a single or re-married father, or someone who has a single or re-married father in their life. Whether you are a father, a step-mother, or a grandparent, or serve another role in the life of the child or children about whom you clearly care so much, you will find something in this book to assist you in ensuring that those children have a better relationship with both parents, and that they are better protected from the emotional maelstrom that inevitably happens whenever a family disunites.

This book is primarily aimed at fathers, because overwhelmingly it is fathers who are pushed out of their children's lives by both the family law system, and society at large. It is often easy to blame the mother as the sole reason that a father is having a difficult time maintaining a relationship with his children after divorce, but it is important to remember that usually that mother's actions are the result of everything she has learned from the family law system, and from whatever her friends and family are telling her. In turn, those friends and family members have learned what they are telling her from societal messages about "how it should be" when a family gets divorced, and about what each parent's role "should" be following a divorce.

Of course, the reality is that children need both parents, and access to both parents, regardless of how the parents feel about each other.

Whatever your current situation, it can always be improved – even the most impossible-seeming situations can be turned around. So don't lose hope, don't lose faith, and, with the help of the information in this book, don't lose your children.

Anne P. Mitchell,
Attorney at Law
DadsRights.org

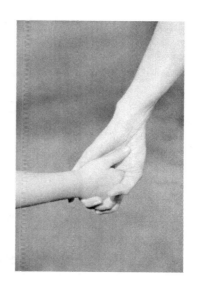

Chapter One

7 Steps to Ensure Well-Adjusted Kids After Divorce

They're Your Kids Too

Introduction

In order to help protect your child from any fallout during the reorganization of your family, and to ensure that your child stays happy and well-adjusted throughout, it is important that you recognize, accept, and even embrace, certain concepts. Sometimes a parent has a hard time accepting these principles, because they run counter to what the parent wants for themselves. It's okay, and even normal, to feel that way; it's just not okay to act on those feelings to the detriment of your children.

The following are some steps which single, or soon-to-be-single, parents can take to help ensure that their children remain on course and well-adjusted, during and after a divorce. These steps may seem obvious to you; unfortunately, what often is not obvious to parents is their own behavior, and how it is perceived by, and impacts, their children.

Step 1: Accept and Acknowledge That Your Child Needs an Active, Ongoing Relationship with Both of Their Parents.

It can be hard, when breaking up with someone, to remember and accept that while you are breaking up with them, your children are not.

No matter how good a parent you may be, and no matter how "poor" a parent you may personally believe the other person to be, your children need both of you. They need to be able to have an unreserved relationship with their other parent, free from your own views of that parent, and unfettered by concerns that you will be hurt, or love them less, because they still want to spend time with their father or mother.

It's your situation, your problem, and your breakup. It is not your children's; don't make it theirs, and don't let it become theirs.

Your children love both of you, and need both of you, even though you may no longer love or need each other. And they need you to understand this, and to be okay with it. Their love for you won't be diminished by their love for the other parent; in fact, they will love you more for making it okay for them to also love their other parent.

In addition to the fact that children need both parents, no matter what kind of parents they may be, there is another very good reason for doing whatever you can to encourage your child's relationship with their other parent: children have a funny habit of growing up. Once out on their own, many children come to recognize that the reality of why they only had one parent around doesn't always match the picture painted by that parent. More often then not, they will come to resent that parent for interfering with their relationship with the other parent.

Step 2: Never Ever Speak Badly About The Other Parent To, In Front Of, or Anywhere Within Earshot Of Your Child.

During the breakup of a marriage, it is normal to have negative thoughts and feelings about the other parent. You may feel that it is their fault that the marriage broke down, or that they are behaving unfairly, or irresponsibly.

It is important that you have an outlet to express your feelings, perhaps a friend, or counselor. But under no circumstances should you express your negative thoughts or feelings about the other parent to or in front of your child! This sort of behavior will lead your child to believe that you don't really want them to spend time with, or care about, the other parent.

Even worse, however, is the message it sends to your child about themselves. It is critical to realize that children are very aware of and identify with both parents. Your child knows that half of who they themselves are comes from you, and half from their other parent.

What does it mean to a child to be told that "Your daddy is a jerk"? Do they think "Daddy is a jerk, but mommy is good"? No! They think "Half of who I am is a jerk, so I must be a jerk too." When a child hears "Your mother is selfish and greedy," that

child thinks "If mommy is bad, then I must be bad too."

This is a very important concept to grasp; few parents would knowingly tell their children that they are no good, and yet every time a parent puts the other parent down around their child, that is exactly what they are doing.

Step 3: Accept and Acknowledge that You and Your Ex Have to Co-Parent Your Children Until They Turn Eighteen.

Regardless of how well or not you and your children's other parent get along, the fact remains that you must co-parent with that other person so long as there are minor children involved.

This is a reality that some separating or divorced parents find difficult to swallow; sometimes, more than anything, they just want that other person "out of their face". But this is not how it works; parents of disunited families will have to interact with each other in some fashion until the children which they share between them turn eighteen, so they may as well make the best of it. You can either spend those years fighting, or getting along. Which do you think is better for your children?

The ideal situation, particularly for the children, who need both parents, is where the parents can come to respect each other as

parents, and work together for the sake of their children. For this reason, it is to everyone's advantage, especially your children's, for you and your co-parent to get to a point as soon as possible where you can communicate with each other respectfully and reasonably.

Sometimes it is easier to achieve this at first with a cooling-off period where you communicate primarily through email if possible, so that you don't have that flood of feelings that a face-to-face or telephone conversation can bring, and which can quickly escalate as you both become more emotional or agitated. Email also has the added advantage of providing a written record of your conversation, to which you can both refer back for clarity about what was discussed.

However you do it, and whatever you do, don't use other people as messengers, and especially don't use your children as go-betweens!

If you find it impossible to have reasonable conversations, even through email, with the other parent, consider co-parent counseling (more about that later), which you can ask the court to order if your ex won't agree to it.

Step 4: Learn to See and Understand the "Other Side".

While in the throes of a divorce or break-up, it is often difficult to see things from the other person's perspective, and to understand why they focus on some things and seem to completely ignore others.

For example, in many cases involving children, it may seem as if the mother's primary concern is financial. But this is understandable when you consider that women in our society are told over and over how men "owe" them for years of gender discrimination and career sacrifices, as well as how all women end up in poverty after divorce, and therefore they have to get as much money as possible from the man. This often plays out heavily in the areas of custody and parenting time, because mothers in most states know that the greater the amount of parenting time the father has, the lower the amount of child support they receive will be.

But it is not the case that these mothers are putting money above what is best for their children; rather it is that they have been led to believe that it's a foregone conclusion that it is best for the children to be with them! Thus, it may not even occur to them that the children need regular, ongoing contact with both parents.

For the father's part, it may seem as if he doesn't care at all about the financial concerns of the mother, and is trying to get as much time with the children as possible in order to avoid paying high amounts of support. This is, however, rarely the motivating factor; in fact, most fathers going through the family law system feel that they must fight tooth and nail for time with their children because they feel as if they are being pushed out of their children's lives. These fathers genuinely fear losing all time and meaningful contact with their children.

It is important to understand that whatever the facts, how each parent sees things is their reality; they truly *believe* their version of "how things are".

Knowing the perspective of the "other side", and what their bottom line is, can greatly help in terms of focusing on what is important, formulating strategy, and negotiating. For instance, many men who are in a position to do so have found, when looking to increase their parenting time, that it works well to offer to continue to pay the amount of child support dictated by the old, lower amount of parenting time, if the mother will agree to a new increased parenting time. By offering to do this, it completely removes the primary incentive for the mother to not agree to increased parenting time for the father (fear of reduced child support), and the amount of child support being paid can

always be adjusted at a later date, if appropriate. Usually a father who offers to do this will find that it costs less to keep paying the old amount than it would cost to pay legal fees to go to court for more parenting time.

Step 5: There Are Some Things Which You Just Can't Do Anything About - Get Over It and Let It Go.

There are many things which are mandatory in family law, with little room for variance. It is important to recognize these things, as fighting them will only frustrate you, and annoy the court. Once you recognize those things which you can't change, you can refocus your energies on those things which you can do something about! As always, laws vary from state to state, and you should check with your attorney for the particulars in your jurisdiction.

Attorneys' Fees: In many states the law specifically authorizes the court to order one party to pay another's attorneys fees in family law cases. The two factors most often considered, in order of emphasis, are I) who earns more money, and II) which party, if any, has brought the case before the court unreasonably. In many such states it is extremely common for a father to be ordered to pay at least part of the mother's attorneys fees, particularly if he earns more than she does, unless she has been extremely unrea-

sonable, while he has been very reasonable, and has attempted to negotiate the issues in good faith. This is another reason to do everything possible to negotiate with your ex first, so that you can demonstrate to the court that you tried to stay out of court, but your ex just wouldn't cooperate with your efforts to negotiate outside of court.

Wage Assignments: It is now the law in most states that a wage assignment (garnishment) for support will be ordered by the court in every child support case. However, in some states the parents may agree that the court order will not actually be served on the paying parent's employer, and thus will not take effect, so long as that parent remains current with the support payments.

Child Support and "Add-Ons": In most states child support is considered to cover just the basics: food, shelter, clothing, etc. The custodial parent is not, and will not be, made to account for how the payments are spent. In addition, the court can, and often does, include several types of "add-ons". The most typical add-ons include the cost of child care, health insurance, and uninsured medical expenses. Where the custodial parent is working, often the costs of child care and uninsured medical expenses are split between the parents.

Taxes: Current Federal law requires that whoever has primary

physical custody gets the tax exemption for the child. Period. It doesn't matter how much support is contributed to the cost of raising the child. However, the custodial parent may, on a yearly basis, sign the exemption over to the non-custodial parent, and in some states the court will order that they do so if the parents agree. Such an order may not withstand a Federal challenge under the Federal Supremacy Clause (which says that Federal law trumps state law) but to date no such challenge has been made. Most typically, with one child the exemption will be alternated from year to year, and with more than one child the exemptions will be split between the parents. But, it is important to remember that the law is that the custodial parent gets the exemption, and for the non-custodial parent to claim the exemption almost always requires that the parents reach an agreement to that effect.

Step 6: Don't Moralize, or Point Fingers.

Most states now have "no-fault" divorce This means that the court is not supposed to consider, and simply does not care about, which party did what. Period. The court is not interested in hearing about your ex's new boyfriend or girlfriend, their going out in the evenings, or their letting the children watch too much television. Similarly, they don't care if your ex feeds them junk food for every meal, or even (usually) if they are letting the kids watch 'R' rated movies.

The court does not want to get involved in what are essentially parenting decisions and, if you think about it, you wouldn't really want them to, because that means that they would start telling you how to parent too!

Trying to make yourself look like the "better" parent by pointing fingers at the other parent will almost always backfire, and make you look petty and controlling. The only way your child's co-parent's activities are likely to have any impact at all on custody or parenting time is if they truly represent a clear danger to the child's safety.

Step 7: Participate in Co-Parent Counseling.

Joint counseling with a co-parent can be very valuable: it provides a safe place for the parents to forge a new, respectful parenting relationship, away from external influences. Sometimes one parent may resist the idea because they believe that the other parent is actually trying to get them into couple's counseling to try to resurrect the relationship, so it is important to be clear when suggesting counseling to your co-parent that this is not your intention. Pre-divorce counseling, which is similar to co-parent counseling, can help a couple facing separation or divorce to dissipate some of the anger and hostility which may lay between them, and assist them in building a better base of

communication. This enables them to work together to make mature, informed, and rational decisions. After all, the decisions which they will make during the course of their divorce will have a profound effect on their children. Furthermore, they will have to continue to communicate in a co-parenting capacity for years to come; the sooner they can reach a place of respectful co-parenting, the better for all concerned, especially the children. Co-parent counseling is not unlike pre-divorce counseling, except that it typically occurs after the initial custody and time-share arrangements have been put into place. Many co-parents find this sort of counseling invaluable as it gives them a place where it is okay and acceptable for them to communicate, for the sake of the children, without the outside influence of the children, second mates, friends, and family.

Conclusion

You are now armed with several important tools and concepts which you can put into practice to help shield your children from the fallout of your divorce, and to protect and enhance your relationship with your children. Use them - your children will thank you.

Unfortunately, sometimes there are specific situations which have already reared their ugly heads (or threatened to do so), and in

those cases, and depending on your individual situation, you may need to take additional steps. These situations include parental alienation, false allegations of abuse, and parental kidnapping. It is critical that you still practice the seven steps you have learned in this chapter, but you will also need the more situation-specific information that is available in the rest of this book.

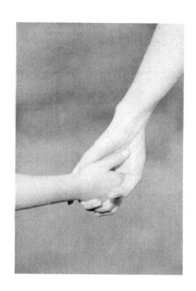

Chapter Two

The Truth About
False Allegations of
Abuse or Misconduct

Introduction

False allegations of abuse of a child, particularly of sexual abuse, or of other misconduct such as alcoholism, drug use, or other illegal conduct, by one parent against the other, are an increasingly common weapon in the divorce and custody arsenal. A false allegation is the perfect weapon. It is simple, fast, and guaranteed to achieve the desired result: the complete removal of the targeted parent from the child's and the accusing parent's life, along with a moral vindication or victory for the accusing parent.

While this chapter specifically talks about false allegations of abuse, as that is one of the most frequent and serious of false allegations, the material in this chapter equally applies to any false allegation, be it of abuse, illegal conduct, or other allegations

Why Do People Make False Allegations of Abuse or Other Misconduct?

Many experts and family law practitioners believe that the increase in false allegations of abuse in the divorce and custody context are a direct result of the move to "no-fault" divorce.

Years ago one had to prove "fault" in order to get a divorce. In other words, one spouse had to prove that the other had either cheated on them, abandoned them, or was in some other way at

fault for the breakdown of the marriage. This led to some rather contrived situations, with one spouse arranging for the other spouse to "find" them in a compromising situation, so that proof of "fault" could then be offered to the court.

Most states have since done away with this fault-based concept of divorce. Many believed that this change would lead to a kinder, gentler system of divorce.

Unfortunately, the advocates of no-fault divorce failed to take one thing into account: human nature. For the most part, people want to be able to point the finger of blame. The fault-based system of divorce allowed the divorce-seeker their proverbial day in court, and an opportunity to prove to the world what a no good so-and-so their spouse was. It gave them a sense of vindication.

By contrast, the no-fault type system of divorce has no such element of good guy versus bad. In many states, one can get a divorce based on "irreconcilable differences". Other states have other, similarly innocuous grounds. There is no longer an opportunity for finger pointing and blame-laying. No longer a path to vindication.

Enter the false allegation of abuse. In one fell swoop the accusing parent can go back to a fault-based system of divorce and achieve utter vindication. With one, unsubstantiated accusation they can often get the targeted spouse completely out of their and the children's lives, and can ensure themselves complete custodial control. And with that one allegation they will completely destroy the other parent's life, and any semblance of a normal relationship between the other parent and their children. As one victim of a false allegation of abuse describes: "It changed everything. My marriage was destroyed. I couldn't see my kids for three months until a psychological evaluation was done. Even after that I could see my kids for only one hour per week up at the courthouse while a probation officer remained nearby. It was totally devastating."

One Allegation, Many Victims

The relationship between a falsely accused parent and child is often not the only relationship which will suffer. Many falsely accused parents find that the allegation not uncoincidentally occurs right around the time that they start dating someone, or they remarry. Few relationships are able to withstand the doubt, confusion, legal battles, and expense brought about by an allegation of abuse.

Business and employment relationships also suffer under the strain of a false allegation of abuse. Many parents lose their jobs after being accused of abusing their children.

Other consequences of the false allegation may, and often do, include loss of reputation, loss of one's standing in the community, and

of course financial hemorrhage. The cost to defend a false allegation may run to the tens of thousands of dollars, particularly if there is a criminal charge involved.

Even for those who can financially afford to deal with a false allegation, the damage to one's reputation, both professionally and personally, can be immeasurable.

The parent targeted with a false allegation is truly a victim in every sense of the word. But the accused parent is not the only victim of the false allegation. For all the pain and devastation which is heaped upon the accused parent, there is often at least as much visited upon the children.

These children will find themselves suddenly ripped from their relationship with the accused parent as surely as if the parent had died; in some ways it is worse than if the parent had died. When a parent dies, a child can usually expect comfort and support from their remaining parent. However the child whose relationship with the targeted parent is destroyed by a false accusation usually finds that the remaining parent is most unsympathetic to the child's loss. After all, it is a loss which the remaining parent themselves orchestrated. Instead of sympathy for the child's loss, the accusing parent will often vilify the other parent in front of the child ("Don't you remember that your father did such and such? How could you want to see him?") More insidious yet, the child who lives with a falsely accusing

parent is often put in the position of having to pledge allegiance
to the accusing parent, sometimes by denouncing, or even im-
plicating, the accused parent. Some children will do this knowingly, but many are too young to even understand this game.
Being trusting and malleable, as young children are, they will
come to adopt the accusing parent's version of what allegedly occurred. In the child's mind, the accused parent becomes as guilty
as if the abuse had actually happened.

Thus, not only has the false accusation created a victim of the targeted parent, but also it will often victimize the child as surely as if the
alleged abuse had actually occurred. And the victimization doesn't
stop there.

A child who is the alleged victim of a false claim of abuse will be subjected to a barrage of interrogations, and to all manner of humiliating
examinations. Young girls are often made to endure painful, intimate
pelvic exams as doctors repeatedly look for evidence of the alleged
abuse, and the accusing parent drags the child from one doctor to
another until they find one who agrees with their allegation. And,
after being subjected to multiple exams by multiple doctors, many
children will begin to exhibit the symptoms of a child who has actually had their most intimate privacy invaded – and small wonder!

Why Is It Still So Easy to Haul Out This Weapon of Mass Destruction?

Given the magnitude of devastation which can occur, both for the accused parent and the child, in a false allegation scenario, why has so little been done to address the issue of false allegations of abuse?

One problem is that it is very difficult to prove that the accuser knowingly made a false accusation - that is, that they knew that it was untrue. For this reason, false allegations usually go unpunished, even in jurisdictions where the law specifically provides sanctions against such actions. Plus, almost anything can be twisted to appear to be a credible basis for an accusation.

Another problem is that many mental health professionals take the "where there's smoke, there's fire" view, and therefore believing that some sort of abuse must have occurred, they set out to prove it.

In addition to it being nearly impossible to prove that an allegation was false, let alone that the accuser knew that it was false, there is a very real and understandable fear that if the allegation is true, and not acted upon, the child will be further abused. Unfortunately, there doesn't seem to be as great a concern that

the children who are the subjects of false allegations are no less victimized than those who may in fact be being abused.

Be Prepared

If the legal system is not going to offer any relief, what can be done to protect oneself against such false allegations? As is so often the case, an ounce of prevention is worth a pound (and in this case, several thousand dollars worth) of cure.

If you are separated, or divorced, and particularly if you are a father (the vast majority of all false allegations are made against fathers), and especially if you believe that you may become the target of a false accusation, you are well advised to take the following precautions:

- Don't allow your child to sleep with you.
- Don't shower or bathe with your child.
- Avoid being naked around your child, and their being unnecessarily naked around you.
- Arrange your parenting time with your child such that you are never alone with your child, particularly if you are in or anticipate a custody dispute. In other words, always have a witness around.
- If your child is of an age where they need as-

> sistance with bathing or going to the bathroom, and particularly if they are of the opposite sex as you, whenever possible have someone who is the same sex as your child assist them, such as an aunt, a grandmother, or a trusted family friend (not your girlfriend!)

The above precautions may seem extremely restrictive. They are. Unfortunately, in the current climate, where false allegations abound, they are also extremely necessary, especially if you don't have a great relationship with your ex. Think about it – which is worse: following the above recommendations, or having all contact with your child cut off because you can't defend against a false allegation (because you had nobody around as a witness, or because your child tells a social worker or judge "I always sleep with Daddy, and we don't wear pajamas")?

How to Tell Whether You May Be a Likely Target

If your child's other parent is attempting to exercise complete control over your child and their relationship with you, and this effort to control becomes more pronounced the more you resist, or whenever the court doesn't see things their way, expect an allegation of abuse.

Also, if your child's other parent was themselves abused as a child, believes that they were abused, or is in therapy for being

a "survivor of abuse", you are a prime candidate for a false allegation.

Many parents are unable to believe that the person with whom they were once involved, that person whom they know "would never do such a thing", would make such an allegation.

Believe it.

Most fathers who are the victims of false allegations could never in a million years have imagined that their ex would make such a horrible accusation.

It is much better to be prepared, than to have to defend such an accusation unprepared. And, should the allegation not occur, the above-suggested measures will have no adverse impact on your co-parenting relationship, as they will be all but invisible to the other parent.

What to Do If You Are Falsely Accused

If you have followed the above precautions, and you do become the target of a false allegation of abuse, you will find it much easier to answer the allegations, and to disprove them. However, despite your precautions, and despite your innocence, and

despite the implausibility or even the impossibility of the allegations, it is critical that you get an attorney immediately, and before you do anything else. Even if the charges are not criminal, your future with your children is at stake. You may feel that you can't afford to get an attorney; the fact is, you can't afford not to.

It is also very important to find a support system. Most parents who experience a false allegation of abuse feel bewildered, alone, and unsure of what to do. They feel as if they are the only person in the world ever to have faced such a problem, and wonder what they could possibly have done to deserve such a horrible fate. In truth, every day there are thousands of parents going through the same thing.

Contact a non-custodial parents' rights organization, and ask about meetings, where you will find resources, support, and understanding.

Finally, once you have dealt with the allegations, be sure to check with your attorney to find out what, if any, legal remedies may be available to you. Although it is very difficult to prove that the accusation was known to be unfounded when it was made, many states do have penalties for intentionally making such false allegations. In some states, the repeated use of false allegations can be grounds for a change of custody.

Conclusion

The best strategy with respect to false allegations of abuse is to realize that it can happen to you, and to take precautions, such as those outlined in this chapter, to head it off at the pass. If an allegation does occur, remain calm, get to an attorney as soon as possible, and realize that you are not alone.

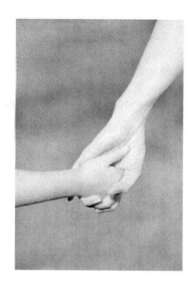

Chapter Three

Parental Kidnapping:
Prepare for it – Prevent it

They're Your Kids Too

Introduction

One of the scariest experiences which a parent can go through is having their child seem to vanish into thin air. Every year more than 350,000 children are abducted by their own parents! This may seem like an extremely high number, and you may be thinking "then why aren't there a thousand abductions a day in the news?" That's because they usually aren't the high profile sorts of abductions where a parent snatches their child and flees the state. They are everyday sorts of occurrences where one parent keeps the child from the other parent.

What is Parental Abduction?

"Parental abduction" is the unlawful taking of a child by one parent, depriving the other parent of their lawful custody or court-ordered parenting time with the child. Parental abduction can be performed by either parent, mother or father, custodial or non-custodial, and can run the gamut from something as seemingly relatively inconsequential as the parent not being home with the child when the other parent comes to pick them up for their court-ordered parenting time, to the much more dramatic situation where the custodial or non-custodial parent disappears with the child.

How Can I Help Prevent Parental Kidnapping?

As we've said before, an ounce of prevention is worth a pound of cure. This is particularly true with parental kidnapping, as once a child has been kidnapped, the perpetrating parent may go underground, or even to another country, and finding the child, let alone retrieving them, can be a nearly impossible task.

First Things First

Every single parent, whether they fear parental abduction or not, should have a valid, current order from the court which spells out the parenting arrangements which they have with their children.

Having a valid, detailed court order for parenting time, which spells out in clear language what the arrangements are, is the single most important thing you can do to help prevent parental kidnapping.

Your court order should be highly specific; if a court order reads only "reasonable visitation" or "parenting time as the parties may agree to between themselves", then it will be very difficult to get the order enforced, let alone to prove parental abduction. For example, if you try to get the police to enforce an order which says only "reasonable visitation", you will have a hard time proving that the order has been violated. If, on the other hand, your court order says "the first and third weekend of every month", and it is the third weekend of the month, and your child is nowhere to be found, that is a clear violation of the order, and you can then get help from law enforcement agencies and the court in enforcing your order.

If you already have a court order which addresses your parenting time with your children, review it carefully to determine how specific it is. If it is not highly specific, consult with an attorney about having it modified. This does not have to be an adversarial process; with the right attorney, a new parenting agreement and order can usually be negotiated cooperatively between the parents and/or their attorneys. After all, having it be specific protects both parents.

Be Prepared

Assuming that you have a very specific parenting time order in place, you have laid a solid foundation to not only help avoid parental kidnapping, but to aid the authorities should the unthinkable occur. In addition, you should take the steps outlined below. All of them will help you to be prepared, and some of them will help to prevent parental kidnapping.

Assemble two sets of the following:
- Several recent color photographs of all children and parents.

- A list of any scars or unusual physical characteristics of both parent and child.

- Two sets of your children's fingerprints.

- A list of all passport numbers, dates of issue, and the countries which issued them.

- A list of all driver's license numbers and the issuing state (both the other parent's, and that of any child who is licensed to drive).

- A list of all automobile registrations, serial numbers, makes, models, and descriptions.

- A list of all credit cards, bank accounts, and social security numbers.

- A list of all the names and numbers of all negotiable instruments, brokerage accounts, and stock brokers.

- A list of all retirement accounts.

- A list of any other tangible assets which are easily converted into cash, such as jewelry, collections, and expensive equipment.

- The names, addresses and telephone numbers of the other parent's family members and close friends.

Keep these two sets of items in two different locations, preferably in the homes of trusted friends or family members. Having two full sets of these documents ensures that if one is not avail-

able, you will still have access to the other.

A safe deposit box is not a good place to keep these items, as banks are not open after hours and on weekends.

You may feel as though you could provide or produce much of the above information at a moment's notice, and so that there is no need to assemble these items, but don't put this off! Even if you are able to keep the coolest head under crisis, and remember every bit of information you need, it is much better to be able to have everything already in order for the authorities, should the need arise.

In this situation, time is truly of the essence. For example, if your co-parent is attempting to leave the country, having his or her passport and identifying information quickly enough may enable the authorities to put a "flag" on their passport in the State Department's computer, keeping them from being able to leave the country with your child.

If You Fear That Your Child May Be Kidnapped to Another Country

If you have good cause to believe that your child may in fact be

improperly taken to another country, you should take the following additional measures:

- If your child has dual citizenship, provide a copy of your court order to the embassy of the country which your child may be taken to, and ask them not to issue a passport for your child.

- Place any passport your child already has in safekeeping, in a secure place which is outside of your home.

- Contact the U.S. Department of State (see "Resources" section at end of this book) and ask that your children's names be placed on a lookout list, and that you be notified if any attempt to apply for a passport for your child is made. If your child already has a passport, which you have in your possession, explain to the State Department that you have the passport in your possession, and that you should be notified of any attempt to apply for a duplicate passport.

If Your Child Is Kidnapped

Despite all precautions and best efforts, you may find yourself in the situation where your child is in fact taken, inappropriately, by the other parent. If you have taken the measures outlined in

this booklet, you are already way ahead of the game, and well-prepared to deal with this situation in a timely manner.

I. If you find that your child is missing, immediately:

- Call the police and file a missing person report.
- Have the police department enter the missing parties' names, description, social security numbers and driver's license information with the National Crime Information Center ("NCIC") to be listed in their computer (criminal charges do not need to be filed to take advantage of this).
- Call Child Quest International. (888-818-HOPE)
- Call the National Center for Missing and Exploited Children. (800-THE-LOST)
- Check your local post office regularly to see if the other parent has put in a change of address form, indicating their new address.
- Immediately upon determining where your child is, contact an attorney in that area, and have them prepare a complaint seeking a Writ of Habeas Corpus, giving the authorities in that state the right to take possession of your child and bring them to the court.

II. If your child has been kidnapped abroad do all of the above, plus:

- Call the U.S. Department of State Children's Passport Issuance Alert Program (CPIAP) at 888-407-4747, and request that a "welfare and whereabouts search" be conducted for your child.

- If the country to which your child has been taken is signatory to the Hague Convention, notify the State Department and request that they assist you in obtaining an "Order of Return", under the Hague Convention. (See Appendix D).

Conclusion

As difficult as it may be to contemplate the possibility of your child being abducted, it is far worse to find yourself dealing with your child actually vanishing, and not being prepared or able to adequately assist the authorities.

Following the steps outlined in this chapter will not only ensure that you are well-prepared should your child be abducted by their other parent, but it may even help to ensure that it doesn't happen.

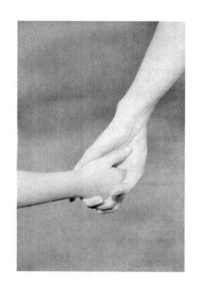

Chapter Four

Parental Alienation:
When "He Said, She Said"
Becomes "He's Gone, She Won"

Introduction

Parental Alienation, or Parental Alienation Syndrome (or "PAS", as it is often abbreviated), is increasingly being recognized as a real, legitimate issue in divorce, custody, and post-divorce situations.

Just What Is Parental Alienation?

First identified as "parental alienation" by Dr Richard Gardner, an M.D. psychologist at Columbia University, Parental Alienation is defined as "the programming of the child by one parent using a campaign of denigration directed against the other." While many, including women's groups and even some psychologists have tried to discredit Dr. Gardner, who passed away in 2003, few can dispute that campaigns of denigration, in which one parent belittles, criticizes, insults, and vilifies the other parent, happen all the time. And it is always the children who come out the losers in these situations, as their relationship with the alienated parent is destroyed, often forever.

Typically the goal of a parent who is guilty of parental alienation is to have the alienated parent removed completely from their own and their children's lives - to end up with sole custody, and being able to exercise complete and absolute control over their children, and any remaining relationship that the child may have with the other parent - if indeed any such relationship survives.

Parents who have had their children alienated from them - the overwhelming majority of whom are fathers - often go for years at a time - sometimes even a whole lifetime - without ever seeing their children. In fact, it can be as if they are dead to their children. For the child, it's actually worse than their being dead: typically if a divorced parent dies, the surviving parent will at least offer some sympathy to the grieving child. But if a child who has been alienated from their father says that they miss their father, or speaks kindly of him, the remaining parent will often be very unsympathetic, if not downright angry or hostile. "How could you miss him when he hasn't seen you in 3 years?", they may say, completely ignoring the fact that they are the reason that their child has not been able to see their other parent.

Recognition by the Courts

Many courts in many states now recognize parental alienation as a serious problem, and, in fact, in some states, if parental alienation is proven, the remedy can include switching custody of the children away from the alienating parent, and to the parent who was being targeted with the alienation.

As a result, the backlash against the introduction of evidence of parental alienation during a custody dispute has risen to the point that in some states, notably California, women's groups

are backing the introduction of legislation which would forbid a court from allowing any mention of parental alienation.

Fortunately for the thousands of children and non-custodial parents who are the victims of parental alienation every day, we do not, yet, at least, live in a country where one cannot raise the issue of parental alienation.

That said, demonstrating to the court that parental alienation is going on requires proof of several factors, some of which are somewhat subjective, making proving parental alienation all the more difficult. For this reason, if you are experiencing parental alienation, you need to move carefully, and methodically, and you must have an attorney who is experienced in parental alienation cases. Ideally you will also be able to move the court to order joint counseling for you and your children, to help them to deal with the vicious programming that they will likely have received at the hands of the alienating parent.

How to Deal with Parental Alienation

The first step in documenting parental alienation is to keep a simple diary or journal, or calendar, in which you make note of any time an alienating event occurs. Obstructing or otherwise interfering with the non-custodial parent's parenting time, in-

sulting or complaining about the non-custodial parent in front of the child, or making false accusations of misdeeds or illegal activities on the part of the non-custodial parent, are all alienating behaviors.

You need to prove a pattern of these behaviors; a custodial parent's interfering with the non-custodial parent's time once, or getting in an argument with the non-custodial parent in front of the child and saying nasty things, while very unfortunate, does not parental alienation make.

But if there is a repeated, observable pattern of these behaviors, it's a pretty good bet that parental alienation is going on, whether intentional or not. And that is an important point - it almost doesn't matter whether the alienating parent intends their behaviors to alienate, because the end result for the child (and the other parent) is the same: the breakdown of the relationship between the child and the alienated parent.

It is also important, during the time that you are documenting these behaviors, that you don't get into it with the other parent. That will only serve to either escalate things, or to cause the other parent to become more subversive and go underground with their efforts, or both. Just calmly register your request to the other parent to not engage in such behaviors, set the record

straight (again, calmly) if possible with your child, and document the date, the behavior, and the outcome, such as:

> *December 25th, 2010 - Showed up for my court-ordered time with my daughter, they weren't home, ex said "Oh, I took her skiing because I knew she'd rather do that then spend the day with you."*
>
> *December 26th, 2010 - Tried to call my daughter, ex said "She's busy with her new presents."*
>
> *January 1st, 2011 - Was supposed to have New Years breakfast with my daughter. Ex said "She's sleeping in after a late New Year's Eve. She needs her sleep and can't go."*

Your (experienced!) lawyer will know when you have collected enough documentation to file a motion with the court. At that point, your attorney should file a motion requesting that the court enforce your parenting time with your child, and letting the court know that you believe that your ex's interference with your time with your children is part of a concerted effort on the part of your ex to interfere with your relationship with your child, and to alienate your child away from you. You should not at this time request a change of custody, or even that your ex be punished, because that will just make you look like you are in it to hurt your ex, when your real goal is simply to protect your

relationship with your child.

The court will often look for certain key indicators of alienation, and in some courts these factors must be present before there can be a judicial finding of Parental Alienation. These factors include:

- Denying or interfering with access and parenting time with the child.
- False allegations of physical, mental, emotional, or sexual abuse.
- Fear on the part of the child of displeasing the alienating parent.
- Deterioration of the parent-child relationship between the alienated parent and the child during times that they are apart.

With respect to the last, as Parental Alienation expert Dr. Michael Bone and family law attorney Michael Walsh explain in an article on the subject published in the Florida Bar Journal, "By way of example, if a father had a good and involved relationship with the children prior to the separation, and a very distant one since, then one can only assume without explicit proof to the contrary that something caused it to change. If this father is clearly trying to maintain a positive relationship with the children through

observance of visitation and other activities and the children do not want to see him or have him involved in their lives, then one can only speculate that an alienation process may have been in operation. Children do not naturally lose interest in and become distant from their nonresidential parent simply by virtue of the absence of that parent. Also, healthy and established parental relationships do not erode naturally of their own accord. They must be attacked. Therefore, any dramatic change in this area is virtually always an indicator of an alienation process that has had some success in the past." *(Florida Bar Journal, Vol. 73, No. 3, March 1999, p 44-48)*

That quote, by the way, is a great one for your attorney to include in their motion to the court!

Often, when dealing with a possible case of parental alienation, the court will order that your child (and maybe your ex, and even you) be interviewed by a psychologist to determine whether, in their professional opinion, parental alienation is occurring. If the court doesn't order it, you may want to request it yourself, as your request says to the court "Don't just take my word for it; I'm very concerned and would like to have a professional involved to evaluate the situation." You should work with your lawyer to ensure, if at all possible, that you get a psychologist who is familiar with the issues surrounding parental alienation, and who does not have a bias with respect to mothers versus fathers.

Conclusion

The most important things to remember when dealing with a parental alienation situation are to keep calm, don't lose your cool, document everything (quietly), and bring your documentation to an experienced family law attorney.

And never, ever give up. Even during times that you may be unable to see your children, they'll know that you are trying.

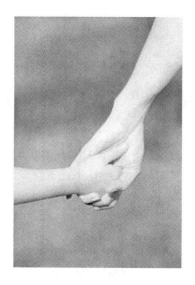

Chapter Five

Resources

The following is a list of resources that you can use, and organizations to which you can turn, if you need support, additional information, or assistance. Included are Kidnap Prevention and Emergency checklists. Remember that having everything in order before something happens can often keep it from happening at all (for example, if you always have a witness with you, that false allegation of abuse is much less likely to occur, or to go anywhere if it does occur).

Appendix A
Helping Children With Divorce

The following books are available at your local bookstore or on Amazon

Putting Kids First: Walking Away From A Marriage Without Walking Over The Kids by Michael L. Oddenino

The Single Father: A Dad's Guide to Parenting Without a Partner by Armin A. Brott

Women Can't Hear What Men Don't Say by Warren Farrell Ph.D.

Mom's House, Dad's House: Making Two Homes for Your Child by Isolina Ricci

Dividing the Child: Social and Legal Dilemmas of Custody by Eleanor E. MacCoby and Robert H. Mnookin

How Not to Screw It Up by Nita Tucker

Appendix B
False Allegations of Abuse or Misconduct

Elusive Innocence: Survival Guide for the Falsely Accused by
Dean Tong

Falsely Accused.com
Law Offices of Patrick Clancy
Century Plaza Towers
2029 Century Park East
14th Floor
Los Angeles, CA 90067
213-531-0504
http://www.falsely-accused.com

Appendix C
Parental Kidnapping

United States of America State Department's Passport Office
877-487-2778

Child Quest, International
1060 N. 4th St. Ste 200
San Jose, CA 95112
408-287-HOPE
http://www.childquest.org

National Center for Missing and Exploited Children
Charles B. Wang International Children's Building
699 Prince Street
Alexandria, Virginia 22314-3175
1-800-THE-LOST
http://www.MissingKids.com

Appendix D
Countries Which Are Signatory
to the Hague Convention

Argentina
Australia
Austria
Bahamas
Belize
Bosnia-Herzegovina
Burkina Faso
Canada
Chile
Croatia
Cyprus
Denmark
Ecuador
Finland
France
Former Yugoslav Republic
  of Macedonia
Germany
Greece
Honduras

Hungary
Ireland
Israel
Luxembourg
Mauritius
Mexico
Monaco
Netherlands
New Zealand
Norway
Panama
Poland
Portugal
Romania
Spain
Sweden
Switzerland
United Kingdom
United States

Appendix E
Parental Alienation

Divorce Poison: Protecting the Parent-Child Bond from a Vindictive Ex by Richard Warshak

Divorce Casualties: Protecting Your Children from Parental Alienation by Douglas Darnall

Douglas Darnall, Ph.D.
PsyCare, Inc.
2980 Belmont Ave.
Youngstown, OH. 44505
330-759-2310
http://www.parentalalienation.org

Breakthrough Parenting, Inc.
2118 Wilshire Blvd. #987
Santa Monica, CA 90403
310-207-9977
http://www.breakthroughparenting.com/PAS.htm

Appendix F
Kidnap Prevention and Emergency Checklists

Kidnap Prevention Checklist 1

Assemble two sets of the following:

- Several recent color photographs of all children and parents.

- A set of your children's fingerprints.

- A list of any scars or unusual physical characteristics of both parent and child.

_____

_____

_____

_____

_____

- A list of all passport numbers, dates of issue, and the countries which issued them.

_____

_____

_____

_____

_____

- A list of any driver's license numbers and the issuing state (including the other parent's, and that of any child who is licensed to drive).

_____

_____

_____

_____

_____

- All automobile registrations, serial numbers, makes, models, and descriptions.

_____

_____

_____

_____

- A list of all credit cards, bank accounts, and social security numbers.

_____

_____

_____

_____

_____

- A list of all the names and numbers of all negotiable instruments, brokerage accounts, and stockbrokers.

_____

_____

_____

_____

_____

- A list of all retirement accounts.

_____

_____

_____

_____

_____

- A list of any other tangible assets which are easily converted into cash, such as jewelry, collections, and expensive equipment.

_____

_____

_____

_____

_____

- The names, addresses and telephone numbers of the other parent's family members and close friends.

_____

_____

_____

_____

_____

Keep these two sets of items in two different locations, preferably in the homes of trusted friends or family members. Having two full sets of these documents ensures that if one is not available, you will still have access to the other.

A safe deposit box is not a good place to keep these items, as banks are not open after hours and on weekends.

Kidnap Prevention Checklist 2

If you have good cause to believe that your child may in fact be improperly taken to another country, you should take the following additional measures:

- If your child has dual citizenship, provide a copy of your court order to the embassy of the country which your child may be taken to, and ask them not to issue a passport for your child.

- Place any passport your child already has in safekeeping, in a secure place which is outside of your home.

- Contact the U.S. Department of State Children's Passport Issuance Alert Program (CPIAP) at 888-407-4747, and ask that your children's names be placed on a lookout list, and that you be notified if any attempt to apply for a passport for your child is made. If your child already has a passport, which you have in your possession, explain to the State Department that you have the passport in your possession, and that you should be notified of any attempt to apply for a duplicate passport.

Kidnap Emergency Checklist

If you find that your child is missing:

- Call the police and file a missing person report.

- Have the police department enter the missing parties' name, description, social security numbers and driver's license information with the National Crime Information Center ("NCIC") to be listed in their computer (criminal charges do not need to be filed to take advantage of this).

- Call Child Quest International. (408-278-HOPE)

- Call the National Center for Missing and Exploited Children. (1-800-THE-LOST)

- Check your local post office regularly to see if the other parent has put in a change of address form, indicating their new address.

- Immediately upon determining where your child is, contact an attorney in that area, and have them prepare a complaint seeking a Writ of Habeas Corpus, giving the authorities in that state the right to take possession of your child and bring them to the court.

If your child has been kidnapped abroad *do all of the above* plus:

- Call the U.S. Department of State Bureau of Consular Affairs at 888-407-4747, and request that a "welfare and whereabouts search" be conducted for your child.

- If the country to which your child has been taken is signatory to the Hague Convention, notify the State Department and request that they assist you in obtaining an "Order of Return", under the Hague Convention (See Appendix D).

Appendix G
United States Directory of
Legal Agencies and Referral Programs

The following is contact information for legal agencies in each state, which you can use to help you find a lawyer for fathers anywhere in the United States.

Generally speaking, when contacting a local bar association or other agency to find a lawyer, it will be helpful for you to briefly explain your situation, why you need a lawyer, and whether you are filing a new case or this is an existing family law case (and if the latter, what stage of the case you are in), so that they can best match you with the most appropriate lawyer. Make sure to emphasize that you need someone who is familiar with and believes in a child's need to have their father involved with his children after divorce.

You should also ask them how they select their referral attorneys and, if appropriate to your situation, whether they have any sliding-scale fee programs or programs for low-income clients, as many state bar associations and other legal agencies do offer such programs. Also be sure to ask about any law schools or other organizations in the area which may offer legal clinics or other practical or financial legal assistance for obtaining representation by an attorney.

Please remember that whenever there are issues relating to custody, parenting time (visitation) and child support, it is always better to try to resolve them between yourselves, or with a counselor or mediator, than to go to court. But it is still critical to have a lawyer who understands the rules, requirements, and pitfalls of the legal system in your area. Your lawyer will act as your guide to help you navigate the terrain and negotiate successfully to arrive at a successful outcome for you and your children, within the framework of the various laws of your state.

ALABAMA

Alabama State Bar Association
415 Dexter Avenue
Montgomery, AL 36104
Phone: (800) 354-6154
www.alabar.org

Montgomery Bar Association
Post Office Box 242551
Montgomery, AL 35124
Phone: (800) 898-2034
www.ala-lawyers.org

Alabama Legal Help
207 Montgomery Street, Suite 500
Montgomery, AL 36104
Phone: (800) 844-5342
www.alabamalegalhelp.org

Legal Services Alabama
207 Montgomery Street, Suite 1200
Montgomery, AL 36104
Phone: (334) 223-0240
www.legalservicesalabama.org

Birmingham Volunteer Lawyers Program
2021 2nd Avenue North
Birmingham, AL 35203
Phone: (205) 251-8006
www.vlpbirmingham.org

Mobile Bar Association
153 Government Street
Mobile, AL 36602
Phone: (251) 433-9790
www.mobilebar.com

Mobile Bar Association Volunteer Lawyers Program

56 St. Joseph Street, Suite 312
Mobile, AL 36602
Phone: (251) 438-1102
www.vlpmobile.org

Madison County Volunteer Lawyers Program

111-A N. Jefferson Street
Huntsville, AL 35804
Phone: (256) 539-2275
www.vlpmadisoncounty.com

ALASKA

Alaska Bar Association

550 W. 7th Avenue, Suite 1900
Anchorage, AK 99501
Phone: (907) 272-7469
www.alaskabar.org

Alaska Legal Services

1016 W. Sixth Avenue, Suite 200
Anchorage, AK 99501
Phone: (907) 272-9431
www.alsc-law.org

Anchorage Bar Association
P.O. Box 100362
Anchorage, AK 99501
Phone: (907) 277-1249
www.anchoragebarassociation.org

ARIZONA

State Bar of Arizona
4201 N. 24th Street, Suite 200
Phoenix, AZ 85016
Phone: (866) 482-9227
www.azbar.org

Arizona Foundation for Legal Services and Education
4201 N. 24th Street, Suite 210
Phoenix, AZ 85016
Phone: (866) 637-5341
www.azlawhelp.org

Maricopa County Bar Association
303 E. Palm Lane
Phoenix, AZ 85004
Phone: (602) 257-4200
www.maricopabar.org

Pima County Bar Association
177 N. Church Avenue, Suite 101
Tucson, AZ 85701
Phone: (520) 623-8258
www.pimacountybar.org

DNA People's Legal Services
201 E. Birch Avenue, Suite 5
Flagstaff, AZ 86001
Phone: (928) 774-0653
www.nativelegalnet.org

Southern Arizona Legal Aid
5658 Highway 260 15
Lakeside, AZ 85929
Phone: (928) 537-8383
www.sazlegalaid.org

They're Your Kids Too

ARKANSAS

Arkansas Bar Association
2224 Cottondale Lane
Little Rock, AR 72202
Phone: (800) 609-5668
www.arkbar.com

Arkansas Legal Services
303 W. Capitol Avenue, Suite 200
Little Rock, AR 72201
Phone: (800) 952-9243
www.arlegalservices.org

Ozark Legal Services Pro Bono Project
4083 N. Shiloh Drive, Suite 3
Fayetteville, AR 72703
Phone: (501) 442-0600

CALIFORNIA

State Bar of California
180 Howard Street
San Francisco, CA 94105
Phone: (415) 538-2000
www.calbar.ca.gov

Legal Aid Association of California
433 California Street, Suite 815
San Francisco, CA 94104
Phone: (415) 834-0100
www.calegaladvocates.org

San Francisco Bar Association
Volunteer Legal Services Program
301 Battery Street, 3rd Floor
San Francisco, CA 94111
Phone: (415) 982-1600
www.sfbar.org/vlsp

They're Your Kids Too

Sonoma County Bar Association
37 Old Courthouse Square, Suite 100
Santa Rosa, CA 95404
Phone: (707) 546-5297
www.sonomacountybar.org

Alameda County Bar Association
610 Sixteenth Street, Suite 426
Oakland, CA 94612
Phone: (510) 893-7160
www.acbanet.org

Bay Area Legal Aid
1735 Telegraph Avenue
Oakland, CA 94612
Phone: (510) 663-4744
www.baylegal.org

BWA Legal Advocacy Program
PO Box 6556
Concord, CA 94524
Phone: (925) 676-3122

Contra Costa County Bar Association
704 Main Street
Martinez, CA 94553
Phone: (925) 686-6900
www.cccba.org

San Joaquin County Bar Association
20 North Sutter Street, Suite 300
Stockton, CA 95202
Phone: (209) 948-4620
www.sjcbar.org

Sacramento County Bar Association
1329 Howe Avenue, Suite 100
Sacramento, CA 95825
Phone: (916) 564-6707
www.sacbarlawyer.org

Legal Services of Northern California
517 12th Street
Sacramento, CA 95814
Phone: (916) 551-2150
www.lsnc.net

They're Your Kids Too

Santa Clara County Bar Association
31 N. Second Street, 4th Floor
San Jose, CA 95113
Phone: (408) 971-6822
www.sccba.com

San Fernando Valley Bar Association
21250 Califa Street, Suite 113
Woodland Hills, CA 91367
Phone: (818) 227-0490
www.sfvba.org

Beverly Hills Bar Association
300 S. Beverly Drive, Suite 201
Beverly Hills, CA 90212
Phone: (310) 601-2422
www.bhba.org

San Gabriel Valley Lawyer Referral Service
1175 East Garvey Avenue, Suite 105
Covina, CA 91724
Phone: (877) 487-3337
www.sgvlawyer.org

Orange County Bar Association
P.O. Box 6130
Newport Beach, CA 92658
Phone: (877) 257-4762
www.ocbar.org

Legal Aid Society of Orange County
2101 N. Tustin Avenue
Santa Ana, CA 92705
Phone: (800) 834-5001
www.legal-aid.com

Ventura County Bar Association
4475 Market Street, Suite B
Ventura, CA 93003
Phone: (805) 650-7599
www.vcba.org

Public Law Center
601 Civic Center Drive West
Santa Ana, CA 92701
Phone: (714) 541-1010
www.publiclawcenter.org

Inland Counties Legal Services
1040 Iowa Avenue, Suite 109
Riverside, CA 92507
Phone: (909) 368-2555
www.inlandlegal.org

Neighborhood Legal Services of Los Angeles County
1102 E. Chevy Chase Drive
Glendale, CA 91205
Phone: (818) 896-5211
www.nls-la.org

Los Angeles County Bar Association Lawyer Referral
1055 W. Seventh Street, Suite 2700
Los Angeles, CA 90017
Phone: (213) 243-1525
www.smartlaw.org

Legal Aid Foundation of Los Angeles
1102 South Crenshaw Boulevard
Los Angeles, CA 90019
Phone: (800) 399-4529
www.lafla.org

Harriett Buhai Center for Family Law

3250 Wilshire Boulevard, Suite 710
Los Angeles, CA 90010
Phone: (213) 388-7505
www.hbcfl.org

San Diego County Bar Association

1333 Seventh Avenue
San Diego, CA 92101
Phone: (800) 464-1529
www.sdcba.org

Bar Association of Northern San Diego County

249 S. Indiana Avenue
Vista, CA 92083
Phone: (760) 758-4755
www.lawreferral.org

Legal Aid Society of San Diego

110 South Euclid Avenue
San Diego, CA 92114
Phone: (877) 534-2524
www.lassd.org

COLORADO

Colorado Bar Association
1900 Grant Street, 9th Floor
Denver, CO 80203
Phone: (303) 860-1115
www.cobar.org

Denver Bar Association
1900 Grant Street, 9th Floor
Denver, CO 80203
Phone: (800) 332-6736
www.denbar.org

Colorado Legal Services
1905 Sherman Street, Suite 400
Denver, CO 80203
Phone: (303) 837-1321
www.coloradolegalservices.org

Metro Volunteer Lawyers
1905 Sherman Street
Denver, CO 80203
Phone: (303) 871-6140
www.metrovolunteerlawyers.org

Boulder County Bar Association
1942 Broadway, Suite 205
Boulder, CO 80302
Phone: (303) 440-4758
www.boulder-bar.org

Metropolitan Lawyer Referral Service
Referrals online and by telephone
Phone: (877) 283-8145
www.mlrsonline.org

CONNECTICUT

Connecticut Bar Association
30 Bank Street
New Britain, CT 06051
Phone: (860) 223-4400
www.ctbar.org

Statewide Legal Services of Connecticut
425 Main Street., 4th Floor
Middletown, CT 06457
Phone: (800) 453-3320
www.slsct.org

They're Your Kids Too

Connecticut Legal Services
62 Washington Street
Middletown, CT 06457
Phone: (830) 344-0447
www.connlegalservices.org

New Haven County Bar Association
PO Box 1441
New Haven, CT 06506
Phone: (203) 562-5750
www.newhavenbar.org

DELAWARE

Delaware Volunteer Legal Services
P.O. Box 7306
Wilmington, DE 19803
Phone: (800) 773-0606
www.dvls.org

Legal Services Corporation of Delaware
100 West 10th Street, Suite 203
Wilmington, DE 19801
Phone: (302) 575-0408
www.lscd.com

DISTRICT OF COLUMBIA (WASHINGTON, DC)

Bar Association of The District of Columbia
1016 16th Street NW, Suite 101
Washington, DC 20036
Phone: (202) 296-7845
www.badc.org

DC Bar Divorce Clinic
1101 K Street NW, Suite 200
Washington, DC 20005
Phone: (202) 737-4700
www.dcbar.org

Corporate Pro Bono
600 New Jersey Avenue NW
Washington, DC 20001
Phone: (202) 662-9699
www.cpbo.org

Hispanic Bar Association of D.C.
P.O. Box 1011
Washington, DC 20013
Phone: (202) 388-4990
www.hbadc.org

FLORIDA

Florida Bar Association
651 E. Jefferson Street
Tallahassee, FL 32399
Phone: (800) 342-8011
www.floridabar.org

Legal Aid Offices of Florida
2425 Torreya Drive
Tallahassee, FL 32303
Phone: (850) 385-7900
www.floridalegal.org

Legal Services of North Florida
2119 Delta Boulevard
Tallahassee, FL 32209
Phone: (850) 385-9007
www.lsnf.org

Legal Services of Greater Miami
3000 Biscayne Boulevard, Suite 500
Miami, FL 33137
Phone: (305) 576-0080
www.lsgmi.org

Bay Area Legal Services

Riverbrook Center, 2nd Floor
829 W. Martin Luther King Jr.
Tampa, FL 33603
Phone: (813) 232-1343
www.bals.org

Broward County Bar Association

1051 SE Third Avenue
Fort Lauderdale, FL 33316
Phone: (954) 764-8040
www.browardbar.org

Jacksonville Bar Association

841 Prudential Drive, Suite 1320
Jacksonville, FL 32207
Phone: (904) 399-4486
www.jaxbar.org

Community Legal Services of Mid-Florida

128-A Orange Avenue
Daytona Beach, FL 32114
Phone: (386) 255-6573
www.clsmf.org

They're Your Kids Too

Florida Rural Legal Services
3210 Cleveland Avenue
Fort Meyers, FL 33902
Phone: (239) 334-4554
www.frls.org

Three Rivers Legal Services
901 NW 8th Avenue, Suite D-5
Gainesville, FL 32601
Phone: (800) 372-0936
www.trls.org

Coast to Coast Legal Aid of South Florida
491 North State Road 7
Plantation, FL 33317
Phone: (954) 736-2400
www.legalaid.org

Brevard County Legal Aid
1017 Florida Avenue S
Rockledge, FL 32955
Phone: (407) 631-2500
www.brevardcountylegalaid.org

Legal Aid Society of the Orange County Bar Association
100 E Robinson Street
Orlando, FL 32801
Phone: (407) 841-8310
www.legalaidocba.org

Legal Aid Society of Palm Beach County
423 Fern Street, Suite 200
West Palm Beach, FL 33401
Phone: (561) 655-8944
www.legalaidpbc.org

Community Law Program
501 1st Avenue North, Room 512
Saint Petersburg, FL 33701
Phone: (727) 582-7402
www.lawprogram.org

Gulfcoast Legal Services
314 South Missouri Avenue, Suite 1C9
Clearwater, FL 33756
Phone: (727) 443-0657
www.gulfcoastlegal.org

They're Your Kids Too

GEORGIA

State Bar of Georgia
104 Marietta Street NW, Suite 100
Atlanta, GA 30303
Phone: (800) 334-6865
www.gabar.org

Georgia Legal Services Program
104 Marietta Street NW, Suite 250
Atlanta, GA 30303
Phone: (800) 498-9469
www.glsp.org

Atlanta Bar Association
229 Peachtree Street NE, Suite 400
Atlanta, GA 30303
Phone: (404) 521-0781
www.atlantabar.org

Cobb County Bar Association
30 Waddell Street, Suite 601
Marietta, GA 30090
Phone: (770) 424-2947
www.cobbcountybar.org

Macon Bar Association
P. O. Box 123
Macon, GA 31202
Phone: (478) 745-1337
www.maconbar.org

DeKalb Volunteer Lawyers Foundation
315 W. Ponce De Leon Avenue, #561
Decatur, GA 30030
Phone: (404) 373-0865
www.dekalbprobono.org

HAWAII

Hawaii State Bar Association
1100 Alakea Street, Suite 1000
Honolulu, HI 96813
Phone: (808) 537-9140
www.hsba.org

Legal Aid Society of Hawaii
924 Bethel Street
Honolulu, HI 96813
Phone: (800) 499-4302
www.legalaidhawaii.org

Volunteer Legal Services of Hawaii
545 Queen Street, Suite 100
Honolulu, HI 96813
Phone: (808) 528-7046
www.vlsh.org

IDAHO

**Idaho State Bar Association
Volunteer Lawyers Program**
525 W. Jefferson Street
Boise, ID 83702
Phone: (800) 221-3295
www.isb.idaho.gov

Idaho Legal Aid Services
310 N. 5th Street
Boise, ID 83702
Phone: (208) 336-8980
www.idaholegalaid.org

ILLINOIS

Illinois Bar Association
424 S. Second Street
Springfield, IL 62701
Phone: (800) 252-8908
www.isba.org

Illinois Lawyer Finder
424 S. Second Street
Springfield, IL 62701
Phone: (800) 922-8757
www.illinoislawyerfinder.com

Chicago Bar Association
321 S. Plymouth Court
Chicago, IL 60604
Phone: (312) 554-2000
www.chicagobar.org

Legal Assistance Foundation of Metropolitan Chicago
111 W. Jackson Boulevard, 3rd Floor
Chicago, IL 60604
Phone: (312) 341-1070
www.lafchicago.org

They're Your Kids Too

Illinois Pro Bono Help
17 N. State Street, Suite 1590
Chicago, IL 60602
Phone: (312) 977-9047
www.illinoisprobono.org

Chicago Legal Clinic Pro Bono Program
2938 E. 91st Street
Chicago, IL 60617
Phone: (773) 731-1762
www.clclaw.org

Cabrini Green Legal Aid
740 N. Milwaukee Avenue
Chicago, IL 60642
Phone: (312) 738-2452
www.cgla.net

Prairie State Legal Services
303 N. Main Street, Suite 600
Rockford, IL 61101
Phone: (815) 965-2134
www.pslegal.org

Champaign County Bar Association Pro Bono Program

1817 S. Neil Street, Suite 203
Champaign, IL 61820
Phone: (217) 356-1351
www.champaigncobar.org

Peoria County Bar Association

110 SW Jefferson Avenue, Suite 520
Peoria, IL 61602
Phone: (309) 674-6049
www.peoriabar.org

DuPage County Bar Association

126 S. County Farm Road
Wheaton, IL 60187
Phone: (630) 653-7779
www.dcba.org

Kane County Bar Association

555 S. Randall Road, Suite 205
St. Charles, IL 60174
Phone: (630) 762-1900
www.kanebar.org

Land of Lincoln Legal Assistance Foundation
8787 State Street, Suite 201
East St. Louis, IL 62203
Phone: (618) 398-0574
www.lollaf.org

INDIANA

Indiana Bar Association
One Indiana Square, Suite 530
Indianapolis, IN 46204
Phone: (317) 639-5465
www.inbar.org

Indiana Legal Services
151 North Delaware Street
Indianapolis, IN 46204
Phone: (800) 869-0212
www.indianajustice.org

Indianapolis Bar Association
135 N. Pennsylvania Street, Suite 1500
Indianapolis, IN 46204
Phone: (317) 269-2000
www.indybar.org

Indianapolis Legal Aid Society
615 N. Alabama Street, Suite 122
Indianapolis, IN 46204
Phone: (317) 635-9538
www.indylas.org

Boone County Bar Association
212 Courthouse Square
Lebanon, IN 46052
Phone: (765) 482-3510
www.boonecountybar.org

IOWA

Iowa State Bar Association
625 E. Court Avenue
Des Moines, IA 50309
Phone: (515) 243-3179
www.iabar.net

Iowa Legal Aid
1111 9th Street, Suite 230
Des Moines, IA 50314
Phone: (800) 532-1275
www.iowalegalaid.org

Polk County Bar Association
625 E. Court Avenue, Suite 100
Des Moines, IA 50309
Phone: (515) 243-3904
www.pcbaonline.org

Linn County Bar Association
P.O. Box 74127
Cedar Rapids, IA 52407
Phone: (319) 365-1212
www.linncobar.org

KANSAS

Kansas Bar Association
1200 SW Harrison Street
Topeka, KS 66612
Phone: (785) 234-5696
www.ksbar.org

Kansas Legal Services
712 S. Kansas Avenue, Suite 200
Topeka, KS 66603
Phone: (785) 233-2068
www.kansaslegalservices.org

KENTUCKY

Kentucky Bar Association
514 W. Main Street
Frankfort KY 40601
Phone: (502) 564-3795
www.kybar.org

Central Kentucky Lawyer Referral Service
219 N. Upper Street
Lexington, KY 40507
Phone: (859) 225-8644
www.fcba.com

Louisville Bar Association
600 W. Main Street, Suite 110
Louisville, KY 40202
Phone: (502) 583-1801
www.loubar.org

Volunteer Lawyers for Appalachian Kentucky
207 West Court Street, Suite 201
Prestonsburg, KY 41653
Phone: (606) 886-8136
www.ardfky.org

They're Your Kids Too

Northern Kentucky Bar Association
529 Centre View Boulevard
Crestview Hills, KY 41017
Phone: (859) 781-1300
www.nkybar.com

LOUISIANA

Louisiana State Bar Association
601 St. Charles Avenue
New Orleans, LA 70130
Phone: (800) 421-5722
www.lsba.org

New Orleans Legal Assistance
1010 Common Street, Suite 1400A
New Orleans, LA 70112
Phone: (504) 529-1000
www.nolac.org

The Pro Bono Project
615 Baronne Street, Suite 201
New Orleans, LA 70113
Phone: (504) 581-4043
www.probono-no.org

New Orleans Bar Association
650 Poydras Street, Suite 1505
New Orleans, LA 70130
Phone: (504) 525-7453
www.neworleansbar.org

Baton Rouge Bar Association
544 Main Street
Baton Rouge, LA 70802
Phone: (225) 344-9926
www.brba.org

Louisiana Legal Forums
4911 S. Sherwood Forest Boulevard
Baton Rouge, LA 70816
Phone: (225) 293-9471
www.la-legal.com

Capital Area Legal Services
200 Third Street
Baton Rouge, LA 70801
Phone: (800) 256-1900
www.calscla.org

They're Your Kids Too

Shreveport Bar Association
PO Box 2122
Shreveport, LA 71166
Phone: (318) 222-3643
www.shreveportbar.com

Legal Services of North Louisiana
720 Travis Street
Shreveport, LA 71101
Phone: (800) 826-9265
www.lsnl.org

Lafayette Parish Bar Association
2607 Johnston Street
Lafayette, LA 70503
Phone: (337) 237-4700
www.lafayettebar.org

Acadiana Legal Services
1020 Surrey Street
Lafayette, LA 70502
Phone: (800) 256-1175
www.la-law.org

Southeast Louisiana Legal Services
1200 Derek Drive, Suite 100
Hammond, LA 70404
Phone: (800) 349-0886
www.slls.org

MAINE

Maine Bar Association
124 State Street
Augusta, ME 04330
Phone: (207) 622-7523
www.mainebar.org

Maine Volunteer Lawyer Project
P.O. Box 547
Portland ME 04112
Phone: (800) 442-4293
www.vlp.org

Pine Tree Legal Assistance
88 Federal Street
Portland, ME 04112
Phone: (207) 774-8211
www.ptla.org

Cumberland Legal Aid Clinic
246 Deering Avenue
Portland, ME 04102
Phone: (207) 780-4355
www.mainelaw.maine.edu/programs-centers/clac.html

MARYLAND

Maryland State Bar Association
520 W. Fayette Street
Baltimore, MD 21201
Phone: (401) 685-7878
www.msba.org

Legal Aid Bureau of Maryland
500 E. Lexington Street
Baltimore, MD 21202
Phone: (800) 896-4213
www.mdlab.org

Pro Bono Resource Center of Maryland
520 W. Fayette Street
Baltimore, MD 21201
Phone: (410) 837-9379
www.probonomd.org

Maryland Legal Services
15 Charles Plaza, Suite 102
Baltimore, MD 21201
Phone: (800) 492-1340
www.mlsc.org

Baltimore County Bar Association
401 Bosley Avenue, Room 100
Towson, MD 21204
Phone: (410) 337-9103
www.bcba.org

MASSACHUSETTS

Massachusetts Bar Association
20 West Street
Boston, MA 02111
Phone: (617) 338-0500
www.massbar.org

Massachusetts Council on Family Mediation
23 Parker Road
Needham Heights, MA 02494
Phone: (781) 449-4430
www.mcfm.org

Massachusetts Legal Assistance
7 Winthrop Square, 2nd Floor
Boston, MA 02110
Phone: (617) 367-8544
www.mlac.org

Boston Bar Association
16 Beacon Street
Boston, MA 02108
Phone: (617) 338-0500
www.bostonbar.org

Greater Boston Legal Services
197 Friend Street
Boston, MA 02114
Phone: (800) 323-3205
www.gbls.org

Hellenic Bar Association of Massachusetts
35 Braintree Hill Office Park, Suite 404
Braintree, MA 02184
www.hellenicbarassociation.com

**Legal Assistance Corporation of
Central Massachusetts**
405 Main Street, 4th Floor
Worcester, MA 01608
Phone: (800) 649-3718
www.laccm.org

Merrimack Valley Legal Services
35 John Street, Suite 302
Lowell, MA 01852
Phone: (978) 458-1465
www.mvlegal.org

Neighborhood Legal Services
37 Friend Street
Lynn, MA 01902
Phone: (781) 599-7730
www.neighborhoodlaw.org

They're Your Kids Too

MICHIGAN

State Bar of Michigan
306 Townsend Street
Lansing, MI 48933
Phone: (800) 968-0738
www.michbar.org

Detroit Metropolitan Bar Association
645 Griswold Street, Suite 1356
Detroit, MI 48226
Phone: (313) 961-6120
www.detroitlawyer.org

Legal Aid and Defender Association
613 Abbott Street
Detroit, MI 48226
Phone: (313) 967-5555
www.ladadetroit.org

Genesee County Bar Association
315 E. Court Street
Flint, MI 48502
Phone: (810) 232-6012
www.gcbalaw.org

Legal Services of Eastern Michigan
436 S. Saginaw Street
Flint, MI 48502
Phone: (800) 322-4512
www.lsem-mi.org

Macomb County Bar Association
40 N. Main Street, Suite 435
Mt. Clemens, MI 48043
Phone: (586) 468-8100
www.macombbar.org

Legal Services of Northern Michigan
112 W. Washington Street, Suite 1
Marquette, MI 49855
Phone: (888) 228-5590
www.lsnm.org

MINNESOTA

Minnesota Bar Association
600 Nicollet Mall, Suite 380
Minneapolis, MN 55402
Phone: (800) 882-6722
www.mnbar.org

Twin Cities Men's Center
3249 Hennepin Avenue South, Suite 55
Minneapolis, MN 55408
Phone: (612) 821-6424
www.tcmc.org

Hennepin County Bar Association
600 Nicollet Mall, Suite 390
Minneapolis, MN 55402
Phone: (612) 752-6600
www.hcba.org

Central Minnesota Legal Services
430 First Avenue North, Suite 359
Minneapolis, MN 55401
Phone: (612) 334-5970
www.centralmnlegal.org

Mid-Minnesota Legal Assistance
430 1st Ave. N, Suite 300
Minneapolis, MN 55401
Phone: (612) 332-1441
www.mnlegalservices.org

Volunteer Lawyers Network
600 Nicollet Mall, Suite 390A
Minneapolis, MN 55402
Phone: (612) 752-6655
www.volunteerlawyersnetwork.org

Southern Minnesota Regional Legal Services
55 E. 5th Street
St. Paul, MN 55101
Phone: (651) 222-4731
www.smrls.org

Minnesota Legal Services Coalition
2324 University Avenue W, Suite 101B
St. Paul, MN 55114
Phone: (651) 228-9105
www.mnlegalservices.org

Legal Assistance of Dakota County
14800 Galaxie Avenue
Saint Paul, MN 55124
Phone: (952) 431-3200
www.dakotalegal.org

Legal Assistance Of Washington County
275 S. Third Street, Suite 103
Stillwater, MN 55082
Phone: (651) 351-7172
www.lawcinc.org

Legal Aid Service of Northeastern Minnesota
350 NW 1st Avenue, Suite F
Grand Rapids, MN 55744
Phone: (800) 708-6695
www.lasnem.org

Legal Services of Northwest Minnesota
1015 7th Avenue N
Moorhead, MN 56561
Phone: (800) 450-8585
www.lsnmlaw.org

Anishinabe Legal Services
411 First Street NW
Cass Lake, MN 56633
Phone: (800) 422-1335
www.alslegal.org

Legal Assistance of Olmsted County
1136 Seventh Street NW
Rochester, MN 55901
Phone: (507) 287-2036
www.laocmn.org

Volunteer Attorney Program
314 W. Superior Street, Suite 1000
Duluth, MN 55802
Phone: (218) 723-4005
www.volunteerattorney.org

They're Your Kids Too

MISSISSIPPI

Mississippi Bar Association
643 N. State Street
Jackson, MS 39225
Phone: (601) 948-4471
www.msbar.org

Mississippi Volunteer Lawyers Project
PO Box 2168
Jackson, MS 39225
Phone: (601) 960-9577
www.mvlp.net

Mississippi Legal Services
2305 5th Street, Suite 2
Meridian, MS 39301
Phone: (800) 498-1804
www.mslegalservices.org

North Mississippi Rural Legal Services
5 County Road 1014
Oxford, MS 38655
Phone: (800) 898-8731
www.nmrls.com

MISSOURI

Missouri Bar Association
326 Monroe Street
Jefferson City, MO 65102
Phone: (573) 635-4128
www.mobar.org

Legal Services of Eastern Missouri
4232 Forest Park Avenue
St. Louis, MO 63108
Phone: (800) 444-0514
www.lsem.org

Bar Association of Metropolitan St. Louis
720 Olive Street, Suite 2900
St. Louis, MO 63101
Phone: (314) 421-4134
www.bamsl.org

Legal Aid of Western Missouri
1125 Grand Boulevard, Suite 1900
Kansas City, MO 64106
Phone: (816) 474-6750
www.lawmo.org

Kansas City Metropolitan Bar Association
2300 Main Street, Suite 100
Kansas City, MO 64108
Phone: (816) 474-4322
www.kcmba.org

Legal Services of Southern Missouri
2872 South Meadowbrook Avenue
Springfield, MO 65807
Phone: (800) 444-4863
www.lsosm.org

MONTANA

State Bar of Montana
7 W. 6th Avenue, Suite 2B
Helena, MT 59624
Phone: (406) 449-6577
www.montanabar.org

Montana Legal Services Association
616 Helena Avenue, Suite 100
Helena, MT 59601
Phone: (800) 666-6124
www.mtlsa.org

Montana Legal Services
2442 1st Avenue N
Billings, MT 59101
Phone: (406) 248-7113
www.montanalawhelp.org

NEBRASKA

Nebraska State Bar Association
635 S. 14th Street, Suite 200
Lincoln, NE 68508
Phone: (800) 927-0117
www.nebar.com

Nebraska Legal Services
1904 Farnam Street, 5th Floor
Omaha, NE 68102
Phone: (888) 991-9921
www.legalaidofnebraska.com

They're Your Kids Too

Omaha Bar Association
PO Box 11195
Omaha, NE 68111
Phone: (402) 280-3603
www.omahabarassociation.com

NEVADA

State Bar of Nevada
600 E. Charleston Boulevard
Las Vegas, NV 89104
Phone: (800) 789-5747
www.nvbar.org

Legal Aid Center of Southern Nevada
800 S. 8th Street
Las Vegas, NV 89101
Phone: (702) 386-1070
www.lacsn.org

Clark County Bar Association
725 S. 8th Street
Las Vegas, NV 89101
Phone: (702) 333-2258
www.clarkcountybar.org

They're Your Kids Too

Washoe County Bar Association
PO Box 1548
Reno, NV 89505
Phone: (775) 786-4494
www.wcbar.org

Washoe Legal Services
650 Tahoe Street
Reno, NV 89509
Phone: (775) 329-2727
www.washoelegalservices.org

Volunteer Attorneys For Rural Nevadans
904 N. Nevada Street, Suite B
Carson City, NV 89703
Phone: (775) 883-8278
www.varn.org

NEW HAMPSHIRE

New Hampshire Bar Pro Bono Referral Program
112 Pleasant Street
Concord, NH 03301
Phone: (603) 224-6942
www.nhbar.org

They're Your Kids Too

New Hampshire Legal Assistance
117 N. State Street
Concord, NH 03301
Phone: (603) 224-4107
www.nhla.org

New Hampshire Legal Aid
48 S. Main Street
Concord, NH 03301
Phone: (800) 639-5290
www.nhlegalaid.org

NEW JERSEY

New Jersey State Bar Association
1 Constitution Square
New Brunswick, NJ 08901
Phone: (732) 249-5000
www.njsba.com

Legal Services Of New Jersey
100 Metroplex Drive, Suite 402
Edison, NJ 08818
Phone: (888) 576-5529
www.lsnj.org

Essex County Bar Association
470 Dr. Martin Luther King Jr. Boulevard, Room B01
Newark, NJ 07102
Phone: (973) 622-6207
www.essexbar.com

Essex County Volunteer Lawyers For Justice
P.O. Box 32040
Newark, NJ 07102
Phone: (973) 645-1951
www.volunteerlawyersnj.org

Union County Bar Association
2 Broad Street, First Floor
Elizabeth, NJ 07207
Phone: (908) 353-4715
www.uclaw.com

Mercer County Bar Association
1245 Whitehorse-Mercerville Road, Suite 420
Hamilton, NJ 08619
Phone: (609) 585-6200
www.mercerbar.com

They're Your Kids Too

Burlington County Bar Association
45 Grant Street
Mount Holly, NJ 08060
Phone: (609) 261-4542
www.burlcobar.org

Camden County Bar Association
1040 N. Kings Highway, Suite 201
Cherry Hill, NJ 08034
Phone: (856) 482-0620
www.camdencountybar.org

NEW MEXICO

State Bar of New Mexico
5121 Masthead Street NE
Albuquerque, NM 87109
Phone: (505) 797-6000
www.nmbar.org

Albuquerque Bar Association
PO Box 40
Albuquerque, NM 87103
Phone: (505) 243-2615
www.abqbar.com

NEW YORK

New York State Bar Association
1 Elk Street
Albany, NY 12207
Phone: (800) 342-3661
www.nysba.org

The Association of the Bar of the City of New York
42 W. 44th Street
New York, NY 10036
Phone: (212) 382-6600
www.abcny.org

The Legal Aid Society
230 E. 106th Street
New York, NY 10029
Phone: (212) 426-3000
www.legal-aid.org

Legal Services NYC
350 Broadway, 6th Floor
New York, NY 10013
Phone: (212) 431-7200
www.legalservicesnyc.org

Queens Volunteer Lawyers Project
9035 148th Street
Jamaica, NY 11435
Phone: (718) 739-4100
www.qcba.org

Project Hospitality Legal Advocacy Program
100 Park Avenue
Staten Island, NY 10304
Phone: (718) 448-1544
www.projecthospitality.org

Neighborhood Legal Services
237 Main Street, 4th Floor
Buffalo, NY 14203
Phone: (716) 847-0650
www.nls.org

Onondaga County Bar Association
Volunteer Lawyers Project
109 South Warren Street, Suite 1000
Syracuse, NY 13032
Phone: (315) 471-2667
www.onbar.org

Rural Law Center of New York
56 Cornelia Street
Plattsburgh, NY 12901
Phone: (518) 561-5460
www.rurallawcenter.org

NORTH CAROLINA

North Carolina Bar Association
8000 Weston Parkway
Cary, NC 27513
Phone: (800) 662-7660
www.ncbar.org

They're Your Kids Too

Wake County Bar Association
8000 Weston Parkway
Cary, NC 27513
Phone: (919) 677-9903
www.wakecountybar.org

Council for Children's Rights
601 East Fifth Street, Suite 510
Charlotte, NC 28202
Phone: (704) 372-7961
www.cfcrights.org

Legal Services of Southern Piedmont
1431 Elizabeth Avenue
Charlotte, NC 28204
Phone: (800) 247-1931
www.lssp.org

Legal Aid Of North Carolina
301 Evans Street, Suite 200
Greenville, NC 27858
Phone: (800) 682-4592
www.legalaidnc.org

North Carolina Justice Center
224 S. Dawson Street
Raleigh, NC 27601
Phone: (919) 856-2570
www.ncjustice.org

Pisgah Legal Services
P.O. Box 2276
Ashville, NC 28802
Phone: (828) 253-0406
www.pisgahlegal.org

NORTH DAKOTA

Dakota Plains Legal Services
PO Box 507
Fort Yates, ND 58538
Phone: (701) 854-7204
www.dpls.org

Legal Services of North Dakota
1025 Third Street N
Bismarck, ND 58502
Phone: (800) 634-5263
www.legalassist.org

Ohio State Bar Association
1700 Lake Shore Drive
Columbus, OH 43204
Phone: (800) 282-6556
www.ohiobar.org

Ohio State Legal Services Association
555 Buttles Avenue
Columbus, OH 43215
Phone: (800) 589-5888
www.oslsa.org

Southeastern Ohio Legal Services
555 Buttles Avenue
Columbus, OH 43215
Phone: (614) 221-7201
www.seols.org

Columbus Bar Association
175 S. Third Street, Suite 1100
Columbus, OH 43215
Phone: (877) 560-1014
www.cbalaw.org

Legal Aid Society of Columbus
1108 City Park Avenue
Columbus OH 43206
Phone: (888) 246-4420
www.columbuslegalaid.org

Cleveland Bar Association
1301 E. 9th Street, Second Level
Cleveland, OH 44114
Phone: (216) 696-3525
www.clemetrobar.org

Legal Aid Society of Cleveland
1223 W. 6th Street, 4th Floor
Cleveland, OH 44113
Phone: (216) 687-1900
www.lasclev.org

Cincinnati Bar Association
225 E. 6th Street
Cincinnati, OH 45202
Phone: (513) 381-8359
www.cincybar.org

They're Your Kids Too

Legal Aid Society of Greater Cincinnati
215 E. 9th Street, Suite 200
Cincinnati, OH 45202
Phone: (800) 582-2682
www.lascinti.org

Legal Aid of Western Ohio
525 Jefferson Avenue, Suite 400
Toledo, OH 43604
Phone: (877) 894-4599
www.lawolaw.org

Advocates for Basic Legal Equality
520 Madison Avenue
Toledo, OH 43604
Phone: (419) 255-0814
www.ablelaw.org

Community Legal Aid Services
265 S. Main Street
Akron , OH 44308
Phone: (866) 584-2350
www.communitylegalaid.org

Dayton Bar Association
709 N. Main Street, Suite 600
Dayton, OH 45402
Phone: (937) 222-6102
www.daybar.org

OKLAHOMA

Oklahoma Bar Association
1901 N. Lincoln Boulevard
Oklahoma City, OK 73152
Phone: (405) 416-7000
www.oklahomafindalawyer.com

Legal Aid Services of Oklahoma
2901 N. Classen Boulevard, Suite 110
Oklahoma City, OK 73106
Phone: (800) 421-1641
www.legalaidok.org

Tulsa County Bar Association
1446 South Boston Avenue
Tulsa, OK 74119
Phone: (918) 584-5243
www.tulsabar.com

They're Your Kids Too

OREGON

Oregon State Bar Association
16037 SW Upper Boones Ferry Road
Tigard, OR 97224
Phone: (800) 452-7636
www.osbar.org

Legal Aid Services of Oregon
921 SW Washington, Suite 570
Portland, OR 97205
Phone: (503) 224-4094
www.lasoregon.org

Multnomah Bar Association
620 SW 5th Avenue, Suite 1220
Portland, OR 97204
Phone: (503) 222-3275
www.mbabar.org

Marion County Bar Association
388 State Street, Suite 1000
Salem OR 97301
Phone: (503) 581-2421
www.marioncountybar.org

Marion Polk Legal Aid Services

1655 State Street
Salem, OR 97301
Phone: (800) 359-1845
www.mplas.org

Lane County Legal Services

376 E. 11th Avenue
Eugene, Oregon 97401
Phone: (541) 485-1017
www.lclac.org

PENNSYLVANIA

Pennsylvania Bar Association

100 South Street
Harrisburg, PA 17101
Phone: (800) 692-7375
www.pabar.org

Pennsylvania Legal Services

118 Locust Street
Harrisburg, PA 17101
Phone: (800) 322-7572
www.palegalservices.org

MidPenn Legal Services
213-A N. Front Street
Harrisburg, PA 17101
Phone: (717) 232-0581
www.midpenn.org

Community Legal Services of Philadelphia
1424 Chestnut Street
Philadelphia, PA 19102
Phone: (215) 981-3700
www.clsphila.org

Philadelphia Legal Assistance
42 S. 15th Street, Suite 500
Philadelphia, PA 19102
Phone: (215) 981-3800
www.philalegal.org

Allegheny County Bar Association
436 7th Avenue
Pittsburgh, PA 15219
Phone: (412) 261-6161
www.acba.org

Neighborhood Legal Services Association
928 Penn Avenue
Pittsburgh, PA 15222
Phone: (866) 761-6572
www.nlsa.us

Erie County Bar Association
302 W. 9th Street
Erie, PA 16502
Phone: (814) 459-4411
www.eriebar.com

Northwestern Legal Services
1001 State Street
Erie, PA 16501
Phone: (800) 665-6957
www.nwls.org

North Penn Legal Services
65 E. Elizabeth Avenue, Suite 800
Bethlehem, PA 18018
Phone: (800) 982-4387
www.northpennlegal.org

They're Your Kids Too

Bar Association of Lehigh County
1114 W. Walnut Street
Allentown, PA 18102
Phone: (610) 433-6204
www.lehighbar.org

Berks County Bar Association
544 Court Street
Reading, PA 19603
Phone: (610) 375-4591
www.berksbar.com

Legal Aid of Southeastern Pennsylvania
625 Swede Street
Norristown, PA 19401
Phone: (610) 275-5400
www.lasp.org

Southwestern Pennsylvania Legal Services
10 W. Cherry Avenue
Washington, PA 15301
Phone: (800) 846-0871
www.swplsconsortium.org

Westmoreland County Pro Bono Program
218 S. Maple Avenue, Suite 103
Greensburg, PA 15601
Phone: (724) 837-5539
www.westbar.org

RHODE ISLAND

Rhode Island Bar Association
115 Cedar Street
Providence, RI 02903
Phone: (401) 421-5740
www.ribar.com

Rhode Island Legal Services
56 Pine Street, 4th Floor
Providence, RI 02903
Phone: (800) 662-5034
www.rils.org

SOUTH CAROLINA

South Carolina Bar Association
950 Taylor Street
Columbia, SC 29201
Phone: (803) 799-6653
www.scbar.org

South Carolina Appleseed Legal Justice Center
PO Box 7187
Columbia, SC 29202
Phone: (888) 346-5592
www.scjustice.org

Charleston County Bar Association
PO Box 21136
Charleston, SC 29413
Phone: (800) 868-2284
www.charlestonbar.org

South Carolina Legal Services
701 S. Main Street
Greenville, SC 29601
Phone: (888) 720-2320
www.sclegal.org

Low Country Legal Aid

167-A Bluffton Road
Bluffton, SC 29910
Phone: (843) 815-1570
www.lowcountrylegalaid.org

SOUTH DAKOTA

South Dakota Bar Association

222 E. Capitol Avenue, Suite 3
Pierre, SD 57501
Phone: (605) 224-7554
www.sdbar.org

Dakota Plains Legal Services

528 Kansas City Street, Suite 1
Rapid City, SD 57709
Phone: (800) 742-8602
www.dpls.org

They're Your Kids Too

TENNESSEE

Tennessee Bar Association
221 4th Avenue N, Suite 400
Nashville, TN 37219
Phone: (615) 383-7421
www.tba.org

Tennessee Alliance for Legal Services
50 Vantage Way, Suite 250
Nashville, TN 37228
Phone: (615) 627-0956
www.tals.org

Nashville Bar Association
150 4th Avenue
North Nashville, TN 37219
Phone: (615) 242-6546
www.nashvillebar.org

Legal Aid of East Tennessee
502 S. Gay Street, Suite 404
Knoxville, TN 37902
Phone: (865) 637-0484
www.laet.org

They're Your Kids Too

Knoxville Bar Association
505 Main Street
Knoxville, TN 37902
Phone: (865) 522-6522
www.knoxbar.org

Memphis Bar Association
80 Monroe Avenue, Suite 220
Memphis, TN 38103
Phone: (901) 527-3573
www.memphisbar.org

West Tennessee Legal Services
210 W. Main Street
Jackson, TN 38301
Phone: (731) 423-0616
www.wtls.org

TEXAS

State Bar of Texas
1414 Colorado Street
Austin, TX 78701
Phone: (800) 204-2222
www.texasbar.com

Texas Rio Grande Legal Aid
4920 N. Interstate 35
Austin, TX 78751
Phone: (800) 369-9270
www.trla.org

Volunteer Legal Services of Central Texas
700 Lavaca Street, Suite 603
Austin, TX 78701
Phone: (512) 476-5550
www.vlsoct.org

Travis County Bar Association
816 Congress Avenue, Suite 700
Austin, TX 78701
Phone: (512) 472-0279
www.travisbar.com

Dallas Bar Association
2101 Ross Avenue
Dallas, TX 75201
Phone: (214) 220-7400
www.dallasbar.org

National Fathers Resource Center
PO Box 50052
Dallas, TX 75201
Phone: (214) 953-2233
www.fathers4kids.org

Legal Aid of Northwest Texas
1515 Main Street
Dallas, TX 75201
Phone: (888) 529-5277
www.lanwt.org

Houston Bar Association
1001 Fannin Street
Houston, TX 77002
Phone: (800) 289-4577
www.hba.org

Houston Volunteer Lawyers Program
712 Main Street, Suite 2700
Houston, TX 77002
Phone: (713) 228-0735
www.hvlp.org

They're Your Kids Too

Lone Star Legal Aid
1415 Fannin Street
Houston, TX 77002
Phone: (800) 354-1889
www.lonestarlegal.org

Tarrant County Bar Association
1315 Calhoun Street
Fort Worth, TX 76102
Phone: (817) 336-4101
www.tarrantbar.org

San Antonio Bar Association Community Justice Program
100 Dolorosa Street, Suite 500
San Antonio, TX 78205
Phone: (210) 227-8822
www.sanantoniobar.org

Jefferson County Bar Association Pro Bono Program
1001 Pearl Street, Suite 202
Beaumont, TX 77701
Phone: (409) 839-2332
www.jcba.org

UTAH

Utah State Bar Association
645 South 200 East
Salt Lake City, UT 84111
Phone: 866-678-5342
www.utahbar.org

Utah Legal Services
205 North 400 West
Salt Lake City, UT 84103
Phone: (800) 662-4245
www.utahlegalservices.org

VERMONT

Vermont Legal Aid
PO Box 100
Montpelier, VT 05601
Phone: (802) 223-2020
www.vtbar.org

Legal Services Law Line of Vermont
274 N. Winooski Avenue
Burlington, VT 05402
Phone: (800) 889-2047
www.lawlinevt.org

VIRGINIA

Virginia State Bar
707 E. Main Street, Suite 1500
Richmond, Virginia 23219
Phone: (804) 775-0500
www.vsb.org

Richmond Bar Association
707 E. Main Street, Suite 1620
Richmond, VA 23219
Phone: (804) 780-0700
www.richmondbar.org

Virginia Bar Association
701 E. Franklin Street, Suite 1120
Richmond, VA 23219
Phone: (800) 552-7977
www.vba.org

Central Virginia Legal Aid Society
101 W. Broad Street, Suite 101
Richmond, VA 23241
Phone: (800) 868-1012
www.cvlas.org

Virginia Legal Aid Society
513 Church Street
Lynchburg, VA 24504
Phone: (866) 534-5243
www.vlas.org

Alexandria Bar Association
520 King Street, Suite 202
Alexandria, VA 22314
Phone: (703) 548-1106
www.alexandriabarassoc.com

Arlington Bar Association
1425 N. Court House Road
Arlington, VA 22201
Phone: (703) 228-3390
www.arlingtonbar.org

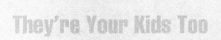
They're Your Kids Too

Fairfax Bar Foundation
4080 Chain Bridge Road, Room 303
Fairfax, VA 22030
Phone: (703) 246-3779
www.fairfaxbar.org

Legal Services of Northern Virginia
6066 Leesburg Pike, Suite 500
Falls Church, VA 22041
Phone: (703) 534-4343
www.lsnv.org

Southwest Virginia Legal Aid Society
227 W. Cherry Street
Marion, VA 24354
Phone: (800) 277-6754
www.svlas.org

Blue Ridge Legal Services Inc.
204 N. High Street
Harrisonburg, VA 22803
Phone: (800) 237-0141
www.brls.org/

Rappahannock Legal Services
PO Box 1662
Rappahannock, VA 22560
Phone: (804) 443-9393
www.rapplegal.com

Virginia Beach Bar Association
2425 Nimmo Parkway, Room C0037
Virginia Beach, VA 23456
Phone: (757) 385-2155
www.vbbarassoc.com

WASHINGTON

Washington State Bar Association
1325 4th Avenue, Suite 600
Seattle, WA 98101
Phone: (800) 945-9722
www.wsba.org

Northwest Justice Project
401 2nd Avenue S, Suite 407
Seattle, WA 98104
Phone: (206) 461-3200
www.nwjustice.org

Washington Law Help
401 2nd Avenue S, Suite 407
Seattle, WA 98104
Phone: (888) 201-1014
www.washingtonlawhelp.com

King County Bar Association
1200 5th Avenue, Suite 600
Seattle, WA 98101
Phone: (206) 267-7010
www.kcba.org

Columbia Legal Referral Services
101 Yesler Way, Suite 300
Seattle, WA 98104
Phone: (206) 464-1122
www.columbialegal.org

Tacoma-Pierce County Bar
Volunteer Legal Services Program
621 Tacoma Avenue S, Suite 303
Tacoma, WA 98402
Phone: (253) 572-5134
www.tacomaprobono.org

Eastside Legal Assistance Program
1510 140th Avenue NE
Bellevue, WA 98005
Phone: (425) 747-7274
www.elap.org

Spokane County Bar Association Volunteer Lawyers Program
1704 W. Broadway Avenue
Spokane, WA 99201
Phone: (509) 462-3701
www.spokanebar.org/

Snohomish County Bar Association
3000 Rockefeller Avenue
Everett, WA 98206
Phone: (425) 388-3056
www.snobar.org

WEST VIRGINIA

West Virginia State Bar
2006 Kanawha Boulevard E.
Charleston, WV 25311
Phone: (866) 989-8227
www.wvbar.org

Legal Aid of West Virginia
922 Quarrier Street, 4th Floor
Charleston, WV 25301
Phone: (800) 642-8279
www.lawv.net

West Virginia Bar Association
PO Box 2162
Huntington, WV 25722
Phone: (800) 944-9822
www.wvbarassociation.org

West Virginia Legal Services
110 S. 3rd Street
Clarksburg, WV 26301
Phone: (800) 401-6439
www.wvlegalservices.org

WISCONSIN

State Bar of Wisconsin
PO Box 7158
Madison WI 53707
Phone: (800) 728-7788
www.wisbar.org

Dane County Bar Association
PO Box 44008
Madison, WI 53744
Phone: (608) 848-1950
www.dcba.net

Legal Action of Wisconsin
230 W. Wells Street, Room 800
Milwaukee, WI 53203
Phone: (414) 278-7777
www.legalaction.org

Milwaukee Bar Association
424 E. Wells Street
Milwaukee, WI 53202
Phone: (414) 274-6760
www.milwbar.org

They're Your Kids Too

Wisconsin Judicare
300 3rd Street, Suite 210
Wausau, WI 54403
Phone: (800) 472-1638
www.judicare.org

WYOMING

Wyoming State Bar Association
4124 Laramie Street
Cheyenne WY 82003
Phone: (307) 632-9061
www.wyomingbar.org